to

from Sally

A BOOK OF ROSES

BY
WILLIAM BRYANT LOGAN

ILLUSTRATIONS BY DREW McGHIE

CONSULTANT
PETER MALINS

William Morrow and Company, Inc.
New York
1984

A QUARTO BOOK

Copyright © 1984 by
Quarto Marketing Ltd.

Library of Congress
Catalog Card Number: 83-62980

ISBN: 0-688-02500-5

A Book of Roses
was produced and prepared by
Quarto Marketing Ltd.
212 Fifth Avenue, New York, NY 10010

Editor: **Bill Logan**
Art Director/Designer: **Richard Boddy**

Typeset by BPE Graphics, Inc.
Color separations by
Hong Kong Scanner Craft Company Ltd.
Printed and bound in Hong Kong by
Leefung-Asco Printers Ltd.

First Edition

1 2 3 4 5 6 7 8 9 10

CONTENTS

To Peter Malins

INTRODUCTION

Adonis, like the Babylonian god Tammuz before him, was a deity without power. Beloved of Aphrodite (her Roman name is Venus), he was raised by Persephone in the Underworld. When the goddess of love asked for the return of her darling, the queen of Hades refused to give him up. Zeus judged the dispute, giving Adonis to Persephone for the winter months and to Aphrodite for the summer. The youthful god was the emblem of being and not-being, of plenty and want, representative of the yearly cycle. His attributes were beauty and youth, exemplified in art by his supple, well-formed limbs and the bloom of his cheeks.

In the ancient Near East, urban dwellers had container gardens on the roof tops of their houses. These mini-gardens were dedicated to Tammuz, from whom the Greeks derived the parallel cult dedicated to Adonis. Four centuries before the birth of Christ, the Greeks were growing roses in small container gardens called "Gardens of Adonis." Roses were grown in other circumstances as well, but their place in the cult of this god is fascinating.

The gardens of the Adonis cult—probably among the first of all gardens that common people could afford to water and maintain—were made to bloom and wither during a very short period, 8 days or less, at the height of the summer. Exactly what part roses played in the Adonai, the festival celebrated at that time, will probably never be known, but they were certainly not intended only as fertility symbols. Let us suggest rather, that they were metaphors for Adonis' yearly career: a period of beautiful and symmetrical florescence followed by a barren and thorny aftermath.

The ancients said lots of silly things about the rose. Pliny, for example, reports that Theophrastus suggested burning rose bushes to the ground each year as a form of pruning. But in the gardens of Adonis, the ancients intuited the way in which roses would be admired for millenia to come: as the perfect, perishing shape of youthful vigor.

Perhaps the most touching use of the rose in early ritual is a similarly two-edged reflection on beauty. Egyptians sometimes would bury the dead with rose chaplets or flowers. From such graves, then and in later times, a rose would occasionally sprout, quite literally "breeding flowers out of the dead land."

Consider the shape of a rose. Almost all of them are built on a calyx of five sepals. If you sketch a figure to join their tips, the result is a pentagram. Curiously, if a man lifts his arms halfway from his side and slightly spreads his legs, he will form the same figure. So the beauty of a man and the beauty of a rose are built on the same structure, a shape which incidentally has been associated with potent magic for thousands of years. The medieval shield, developed to cover and protect the human body but later abstracted in heraldry, often adopted a roughly pentagrammatic form. The rose appears so frequently in heraldry perhaps because it fit this shape, so the rose has in a sense been directly overlaid upon the human body.

Medieval armorers worked the rose into countless abstract patterns for their shields, from a simple schema of five petals to the rose set against a sunburst, the famous "rose-en-soleil" which was Edward IV's emblem during the fifteenth-century War of the Roses. Since the end of the eighteenth century, rose breeders have been making an even greater range of patterns in the shapes of the flowers themselves. True, there were complex roses long before that time. Theophrastus reports a hundred-petalled rose centuries before the Christian era. But these were the result of chance crosses. The nineteenth-century French, in particular, under the influence of Napoleon's Empress Josephine with her famous rose garden at Malmaison, intentionally began to combine strains, essentially by leaving selected roses alone together. (This was called open pollination, something like open marriage, and it is interesting to note that the parents of cultivars were seldom listed in those days.) Not until the beginnings of this century was genetics well enough understood to give breeders an idea of the kind of dice they were throwing when they combined two strains. Hand pollination of one parent (the "pollen parent") on the other (the "seed parent") is the technique that has allowed hybridizers at least to keep track of—and make rough predictions about—the thousands of cultivars so produced. Still, of the thousands of crosses a nurseryman may make each year, no more than a handful will be kept as potential new roses for the market. Intensive breeding in recent years tries for a newer and more perfect combination of the rose's three virtues: shape, color, and scent.

SHAPE. Novel patterns in a rose have always been admired. (Witness Theophrastus' fascination with his hundred-petalled rose.) But only as breeding became an intentional process did the flower's shape enter the domain of fashion. The simplest pattern on a rose's armature of sepals is the single flower of only five petals. It may look flat, star-like, with a nest of stamens at the center, like the *rugosa* roses 'Alba' and 'Typica' in this volume. Or it may be cupped, as is 'Austrian Copper.' The old shrub roses like these—together with the double-flowered hybrids of the Damasks, Albas, Gallicas and Centifolias—are perennial favorites for the garden, and suffer declines in popularity only when the rage for some new rose is at its height. They have their disadvantages: many bloom only once each season, and the flowers appear on stems too short for cutting.

The nineteenth century brought the quest for shape to

the fore. More and more petals per flower was the breeder's ideal. Through the Bourbon roses, the Noisettes, the Damask perpetuals and the hybrid perpetuals, more and more double forms appeared. Some were ruffled like a petticoat, with layers of imbricated petals. The ultimate Victorian roses, like 'Mme. Pierre Oger' in this book, tended to be globose and so full of petals that the inner ones divided into four separate clusters. These are the roses called "quartered."

The breeding of more tea rose blood—derived from the Chinese rose *R. odorata* first imported to Europe in 1809—into late nineteenth-century hybrids led to a set of new fashions that have remained current to the present day. The hybrid tea roses thrust up large flowers, usually singly, at the end of long canes. The bushes are generally less attractive, but the flowers more gorgeous. They were therefore ideal specimen roses, for cutting or for beautifying the garden. If the tendency of centuries of growing was to emphasize the flower at the expense of the bush, the hybrid teas were its ultimate outcome. Even within this class, though, winds of fashion have shifted back and forth. Urnshaped buds have been the rage, only to be upstaged by long, pointed buds or slender, ovoid ones. Today, some are disappointed with a flower if it opens into a mere cup shape, showing its stamens in the center. They would rather see a very full, flat or imbricated bloom, or better yet, a high-centered flower that throws its outer petals into a whorl as though by centrifugal force.

But even the hybrid teas become tiresome. By the thirties of this century, breeders were already paying renewed attention to the bush. The Asian climbers and bush roses, *R. multiflora* and *R. wichuriana*, have now been bred with hybrid teas to produce attractive, cluster-flowering bushes, of little use for the cutting garden but very attractive as bedding plants. They include the floribundas, the *kordesii* climbers and other modern climbers.

Repeated breeding of floribundas with hybrid teas is now producing another class—the grandifloras—whose separation as a class is provoking the same kind of controversy today as occurred in the late nineteenth century over the then novel name, hybrid tea. Members of this new class produce flowers in clusters like the floribundas, but the flowers are larger, shaped more like hybrid teas, and they often appear on long stems. They represent the effort to combine a healthy and attractive bush with gorgeous cutting flowers. What a wealth of inspiration the medieval armorer would find today, if he could see the countless supple patterns that breeders have built on the plain pentagram of sepals.

COLOR. He would also be astounded by the range of colors. The ancient West knew only the white and the red rose. Both are associated with Aphrodite: myth says that the white came into being to clothe her naked body when she was born out of the sea, and that the red is just the white transformed. Running to the wounded Adonis, she scratched herself on a rose's thorn and the blood, dripping onto the white flower, turned it and its progeny forever red. A true yellow rose was reported in Spain in the twelfth century, but it was lost thereafter for centuries. The yellow rose, *R. foetida,* was found in the West in the sixteenth century, chiefly in Austria. Its sport, or mutation, 'Austrian Copper,' combined yellow and copper colors in a single flower. Red-and-white striped sports of *R. damascena* and *R. gallica* were also known in Renaissance Europe. These represented the full color range until 1900.

The break came when the French breeder Pernet-Ducher succeeded in crossing 'Persian Yellow'—a variety of

R. foetida which unlike the Austrian yellows was fertile—
with a hybrid perpetual, producing the first modern yellow
hybrid, 'Soleil d'Or.' (Life does imitate art: Remember that
Edward IV's emblem more than 400 years earlier had been
the Rose-en-Soleil.) From this parent came all the yellows
and yellow bicolors in modern roses.

Three decades later, there occurred an even more as-
tounding event. The pigment pelargonidin, never reported in
any species rose, lent its tones to 'Gloria Mundi' and 'Paul
Crampel' and emerged full-blown in 'Independence.' This
was a lucky throw of the genetic dice, at least for those who
love brightly colored flowers. The color of pelargonidin is
usually described as orange-scarlet, but it really looks like a
luminous and at the same time translucent red overlaid
with yellow. The effect is remarkable, if not downright fright-
ening. Further breeding with pelargonidin-bearing roses has
produced a whole tribe of brilliant flowers. Perhaps the finest is 'Tropicana', a rose so unearthly that some people, see-
ing it for the first time in a vase, refuse to believe in it.

The truly blue rose still eludes hybridizers (though one
may be surprised to hear that anyone would look for it).
There are lilac, purple, even nearly black roses, but no del-
phinium blues. In addition, as some roses age, they
may turn a shade of magenta. Many people regard this as
an unfortunate trait in a modern rose, but it is difficult to
see just why. The only really blue roses are "blued"; long
ago, the Arabs learned to get the color by a simple process:
they injected indigo under the stem's bark.

SCENT. In the rush for novel shapes and colors, scent has
often been left behind. Writers of rose books wax eloquent
over the heady musky perfume of the old roses. In fact,
some of them have no smell at all, but many of the centifolias and musk roses and their descendants are wonderfully

fragrant. When tea roses were first introduced in the West, they were said to have a lighter, less penetrating scent, rather like the scent of tea leaves. One old rose, the important *R. foetida*, has a pronounced and not altogether agreeable smell. The most well-disposed say it smells of linseed oil; others claim it reeks of rotten fruit.

The earliest hybrid teas usually had the light scent of their dominant ancestors. Repeated mixing of blood has meant that today's hybrid teas may be anywhere from scentless to as heady as the most odorous old rose. Early floribundas were almost all scentless, a defect which is still in the process of being eradicated. Recently, breeders have begun to pay closer attention to scent, perhaps sensing that the rush to larger and more sightly blooms is ending.

One rule of thumb to use in predicting a rose's scent is surprising. Given roses of the same class and with roughly the same number of petals, the flower with darker petals will have the stronger perfume!

REMONTANCY. One further factor has obsessed rose growers over the centuries. It has less to do with the physical bases of the rose's grace, more to do with making that grace abundant. The lover of roses finds herself in Aphrodite's position, unwilling to relinquish her darling. The ancient Egyptians had already learned how to make artificial roses, carving them from wood shavings, dyeing them red and adding rose oil for scent. The Romans forced certain roses to bloom early or late, flushing their roots with warm water. The rose which Virgil called *bifera* (twice-bearing) may very well refer to this practice, rather than to a bush that actually bloomed twice in a season, though he may have meant a true remontant variety of *R. damascena*.

No rose native to Europe blooms more than once in a season. Many Asian varieties, particularly *R. chinensis* and

R. odorata, are dependably recurrent. Almost all modern garden roses are remontant because they contain this Asian blood. The earliest crosses combining European and Asian varieties—the Damasks, the Bourbons, the hybrid perpetuals—were not necessarily twice-blooming. It turns out that the genetic trait for recurrence is recessive, so it takes several generations of crosses to select it dependably. In fact, one of the chief attractions of the original hybrid teas is that they were dependably remontant, as are their descendants, the floribundas and grandifloras. The modern rose grower, then, has got a leg-up on the Garden of Adonis. She gets her beauties twice a year, not just once. Buyers of cut flowers can even get a limited selection of hybrid teas all year long, since they are forced in commercial greenhouses.

We are now in a position, however, where all this biotechnology has taken an emotional toll. Progress in the modern classes goes on apace, but one has the sense that their surprises are all past. The private grower seeks to diversify, adding more of the old roses to the garden, even at the expense of twice-blooming exhibition flowers. Breeders search among the species roses for new crosses that may lead to new classes entirely. A BOOK OF ROSES reflects the modern rose garden. Selected by Pete Malins, rosarian of the Brooklyn Botanic Garden and one of the most knowledgeable rose men in the country, the flowers include species roses and old shrub roses, as well as the modern classes. Most roses are notorious for the speed with which they wither once cut. We hope that our rose book will at least mitigate the pain of Adonis' brevity, cheating Persephone by the winter fire and perhaps offering a new rose or two for the summer to come.

William Bryant Logan

ROSE NOMENCLATURE

Modern roses are usually the children of named rose varieties. At least two roses will be listed in every rose's pedigree: its pollen parent—the rose whose pollen was used to make the cross—and its seed parent—the rose whose flower was pollinated. In this book, a rose's parents are listed, wherever possible, in the following form: 'seed parent' x 'pollen parent.' Sometimes, the ancestors of each parent may be further listed within brackets in the pedigree. When the parents are unnamed seedlings, the word "seedling" replaces the variety name. The date appended to each pedigree refers to the year in which the rose entered commerce.

AMERICA

CLIMBER
'Fragrant Cloud' x 'Tradition,' 1976

—

Very modern and clean, America is disease-resistant
and flowers continuously, offering big clusters of
coral-rose blooms, each with nested, overlapping
petals. The flowers look almost like porcelain. The
rose won the AARS trials in 1976. Some people may
be surprised to find two hybrid tea parents
producing a climbing offspring, but America is not
a mutation. Habits of the great climber 'Don Juan,'
a parent of 'Tradition,' are simply
reappearing in America.

AUSTRIAN COPPER

Rosa foetida bicolor

Austrian Copper is a unique rose, beautiful, crucial and difficult. It is almost certainly a mutation, or sport, of Austrian Yellow *(R. foetida),* which Arab invaders reported bringing to Spain as early as the thirteenth century. It was lost thereafter, but was found naturalized in Austria during the 1500s. The sport existed before 1590. Its simple, single flowers are yellowish on the outside and bright orange-scarlet on the inside, growing on lush bushes up to 7 feet high. Gorgeous in itself, Austrian Copper is a member of the same species that produced all the orange and yellow flowers among modern roses. There are two important caveats, however, for anyone who would grow this historic rose: First, it isn't called *foetida* for nothing. The scent is charitably compared to that of linseed oil. Second, it is very susceptible to disease.

BETTY PRIOR

FLORIBUNDA
'Kirsten Poulsen' x seedling, 1935

The Dane Svend Poulsen produced the first floribunda roses during the teens and twenties of this century. Crossing the multi-flowered polyantha roses with repeat-blooming hybrid teas, he got a hardy rose that would survive Scandinavian winters and produce masses of blooms during the short growing season. Betty Prior is a striking descendent of one of the Dane's early successes, 'Kirsten Poulsen.' The blooms are cupped and single—an elegant simplicity not always found in floribundas—appearing in clusters of up to 30 flowers. Each one is carmine- to salmon-pink, sometimes even cherry red. The petal's inside surface is often lighter than its outside, tending to white at the center. Scentless like most of the early floribundas, Betty Prior nonetheless makes an unsurpassed hip-high hedge or bedding rose.

BING CROSBY

HYBRID TEA
seedling x 'First Prize,' 1981

~

Bing Crosby is big, consistent and practically fluorescent. The spring flowers are a bright orange-red, which AARS judges described as similar to a "medium-ripe persimmon" when they gave the tea a 1981 award. Flowers that come later in the year are a deeper color, sometimes red-orange. All have 40 or more petals, ovoid in the bud and arching out in concentric circles as the flower opens. The bush will grow almost to chest height, thrusting its blooms up singly on long, glossy-leaved stems. Bing is a stopper in the rose garden, but it is also an excellent, long-lived cut flower.

BLUE MOON
MAINZER FASTNACHT

HYBRID TEA
'Sterling Silver' seedling x seedling, 1965

~

This is quite an ordinary hybrid tea, really. The flowers are medium-large, double and redolent, standing at the end of long, sturdy stems. Foliage is a glossy green, and the plant grows fairly high and bushy. The flower is purple, of course, or lilac, if it makes you squeamish to think of a purple rose. The Germans named it for *Fastnacht,* or Shrove Tuesday, perhaps thinking of the eerie midnight hour between the feasting of Carnival and the fasting of Lent.

CADENZA

CLIMBER
'New Dawn' x 'Climbing Embers,' 1967

A climbing rose with distinguished ancestry among
the floribundas, the blood-red Cadenza shows how
many different strains can go into the make-up of a
lovely modern rose. The 'New Dawn' parent is itself a
sport, or mutation, but it has *R. wichuriana,* dean of
climbing species, in its ancestry. A striking rose in
itself, 'New Dawn' has passed on to Cadenza its
wonderful habit of blooming profusely and repeatedly
during a single season. Cadenza's other parent has
'Eva' in its background. This seminal hybrid musk
rose has been the progenitor of countless floribundas
and a few fine hybrid teas as well. Cadenza's
urn-shaped buds have a delicate odor, and the
flowers remain a deep red until their petals fall.

CHAPEAU DE NAPOLÉON
CRESTED MOSS

Rosa centifolia cristata
1827

~

The rose was first found growing out of a tower wall at Fribourg, Switzerland, in 1820. The velvety green sepals are what give it the "Crested Moss" name—though it isn't strictly speaking a moss rose—for they bear the "mossy" glands that the true moss rose has all around its flowers. Before the blooms have opened, the sepals fold over them as though to clasp them shut. The buds are most attractive when they are only partly open. Then, the clear pink, very full flowers are still held in shape by their sepals. The plant grows to 5 feet high, flowers but once a season—though for a month at a time—and is very fragrant.

CHRYSLER IMPERIAL

HYBRID TEA

'Charlotte Armstrong' x 'Mirandy,' 1952

~

Chrysler Imperial seems somehow to be the rose of postwar American confidence. It is a rose's rose's rose: not flashy in color or startling in form, but yielding many perfect, dusky crimson, high-centered double flowers, each with a heady scent mixing old-rose and clove. The flower has the solid-steel grace and precision of the fifties American automobile. The same cannot be said of the plant it grows on, which tends to be sparse and ungainly—but who's quarreling? Mildew may spoil the rose in humid climates; otherwise, its spindly canes thrust their beauties proudly forward.

COLORAMA

HYBRID TEA
'Suspense' x 'Confidence,' 1968

~

The name fits the flower: Its petals are golden yellow, tinged with salmon on the outside; inside, they are bright crimson. The foliage is extra glossy. One parent is a descendent of 'Peace,' the other of 'Floradora,' so the plant is vigorous and hardy enough to keep blooming through a hot, humid August. Blooms are shapely and medium-large, about as wide across as a lady's hand.

COLOR MAGIC

HYBRID TEA
seedling x 'Spellbinder,' 1978

~

This lovely bicolor rose is an unusually strong bloomer, all season long. Not even the muggy days of late summer can faze it, as it sends up its ivory-and-crimson blooms singly on thick canes. The bud is long and oval, opening into a flattish flower of 20 to 30 petals. The modest petalage means that the bloom shows off its curves crisply, with the clarity of ripples on a pond. Foliage is dark green, and the plant grows medium high. Its magic fails in only one regard: the flower has no scent.

COMMON MOSS ROSE
OLD MOSS

Rosa centifolia muscosa

～

The Centifolia roses often produce sports, or mutations. The "moss" of these roses is the most desirable of those. Calices, sepals and flower stems—sometimes even the leaflets—are covered with small, upstanding glands, rather like the warts on a toad's back but far more attractive. The glands provide a rough and spiny nest for the smooth, cup-shaped pink flowers that grow in groups of up to five on a medium-sized bush. Some of the blooms maintain an orderly geometrical decorum as they open, while others let their inner petals twist every which way. Old Moss blooms only once a season, but during that time one can hardly imagine a more interesting waist-high hedge plant. Its extra virtues include a powerful fragrance and a winter hardiness that lets it withstand temperatures below zero degrees Fahrenheit.

Don Juan

Climber
'New Dawn' seedling x 'Detroiter,' 1958

◥

Like 'Cadenza', this strong climber gets vigor from its parent 'New Dawn,' reaching heights taller than a tall man. It may well have been named for the ardent fervor with which it sends single, velvet-red flowers up a trellis or along a fence, as though to hand them to a beloved. The brilliant blooms give a most painterly effect, virtually flat on top but with sinuous, imbricated petals. Also like its half-brother, Don Juan blooms dependably, if not as profusely, through the entire season. There is some question as to whether Juan's pollen parent is 'Detroiter' or 'New Yorker,' both full red hybrid teas. Regionalists may argue the point, but whichever the parent was, it left this rose with the light scent characteristic of many hybrid teas.

DOUBLE DELIGHT

HYBRID TEA
'Granada' x 'Garden Party,' 1976

~

Its bud and its strong, spicy fragrance are what sell
Double Delight. The rose blooms with pointed or
urn-shaped buds, showing strong bands of a lively
red, set on an ivory or yellow foundation. Some
individuals bloom ivory with just a thin fringe of red,
some are almost all red. The open flowers average 40
petals each, but they are much less shapely than the
buds. The flower fades to magenta with age,
disgusting growers who think rose gardens should
always look fresh and never clash, like new-pressed
party clothes. Very vigorous and bushy with plenty
of semi-glossy leaves for a setting, the rose has the
added virtue of excellent resistance to mildew.

DUET

HYBRID TEA
'Fandango' x 'Roundelay,' 1960

❦

Hybrid tea though it is—and winner of the 1961 AARS award—Duet bears its flowers in clusters like a floribunda. Petals are light to salmon-pink on one side, with red shades on the reverse. As the large flowers have a ruffled look, the colors blend most pleasantly. The fragrance combines a touch of tea and a touch of old-rose musk. The medium-sized bush, with its dark green glossy foliage, is exceptionally disease-resistant, providing one of the most dependable and late-blooming of the hybrid teas.

ECLIPSE

HYBRID TEA
'Joanna Hill' x 'Federico Casas,' 1935

❧

The great thing about Eclipse is its bud stage when
it has the intense, geometrical beauty of the moon
coming out of eclipse. The long, curving, dark yellow
blossom soon begins to flare sinuously at the peak. It
is a fine rose for the cutting garden, but don't hold
back the shears waiting for the open flower. Though
it is golden yellow and fragrant, it opens too wide
and too fast, and it dies soon.

Europeana

FLORIBUNDA

'Ruth Leuwerik' x 'Rosemary Rose,' 1963

~

Bright velvet, sometimes blood-red, and very full, Europeana is one of the most abundant floribundas. The ruffled flowers bloom in large, heavy trusses, sometimes so numerous they weigh down their stems. The bush is no more than hip-high, but with its glossy dark leaves, it looks very full. To make matters more pleasing still, the flowers give off a scent like a mixture of ripe fruit and tea.

FIRST EDITION

FLORIBUNDA

'Zambra' x [('Orleans Rose' x 'Goldilocks') x ('Orange Triumph'
seedling x 'Floradora')], 1976

❧

Sit down for this pedigree. Now, as we saw with 'Betty Prior', the first floribundas were created by crossing hybrid teas with the dependable and hardy polyantha roses. So a bright breeder, looking for more of a good thing, crosses the floribunda 'Goldilocks' against the polyantha that was first used to make a floribunda cross, the 'Orleans Rose.' Separately, he crosses another floribunda with the seedling of another polyantha, both parents having the famous and prolific rose 'Eva' as a common ancestor. He next crosses the two floribunda–polyantha crosses, and crosses the resulting cross with 'Zambra,' a modern floribunda that comes from crossing a cross of 'Goldilocks' and 'Fashion' with itself. Got it? The breeder gets new blood from old polyanthas and floribundas, while simultaneously working the famous 'Eva,' 'Pinocchio' and 'Crimson Glory' (the last two, parents of 'Fashion') into his rose's lineage. He also gets the 1977 AARS award. Considering the labor, that's the least they could have done! First Edition is a sturdy beauty. Its 30-petaled, coral-to-orange flowers make lovely, high-centered buds and attractive, shapely blooms. They appear continuously in large, plentiful clusters on a medium-tall bush. Not least among its virtues, the plant is unusually resistant to mildew and black spot.

FIRST PRIZE

HYBRID TEA
'Enchantment' seedling x 'Golden Masterpiece' seedling, 1970

~

This rose is a rose that is rose, its color halfway between red and pink. Sometimes it may tend to magenta, have purplish edges or even an ivory center. Its glory is its long, slender bud that opens by exfoliation, each petal peeling away as though carved from wood. Open flowers, by contrast, have a relaxed, rustic look. The plants are very healthy, though a bit sparse.

FRAGRANT CLOUD
DUFTWOLKE

HYBRID TEA
seedling x 'Prima Ballerina,' 1963

❦

Some people class Fragrant Cloud as a floribunda,
since it pumps out blooms in groups of up to five.
But as each double flower may be as broad as a
man's hand, most like to consider it a hybrid tea.
You can clip off the less vigorous flowers of a cluster,
leaving a single bloom to ripen magnificently. The
high-centered bud stage is particularly appealing:
Petals are deep rose pink on the outside and scarlet
within, with a dark purple flush at the base. Open
flowers turn a coral red, fading to purple. The bush
grows only hip-high, but it is very thick and
abundant, full of flowers and dark, glossy foliage.
The word "fragrant" in the name may be slightly
misleading; "pungent" might be better.

FRITZ NOBIS

Rosa rubiginosa hybrid
'Joanna Hill' x 'Magnifica,' 1940

~

The *rubiginosa* (or *eglanteria*) species is a wonderful producer of tall shrub roses, and unlike most of the roses found in modern gardens, it is native to Europe. The plants are generally graceful, arching, and loaded with flowers. Imagine what happens when a rose of this character is successfully crossed with a hybrid tea like 'Joanna Hill': Fritz Nobis will grow up to 12 feet tall with arched canes and a strong, distinctive fragrance. Up to 20 blossoms may appear in a single cluster...but they are big, gorgeous hybrid tea blossoms! White within and a yellowish-pink outside, the flowers are backed by copious light green leaves. The plant is disease-resistant and hardy down to about five degrees Fahrenheit. As more and more people rediscover the hardy shrub roses, Fritz Nobis ought to be among their happier surprises.

GOLD MEDAL

GRANDIFLORA

'Yellow Pages' x ('Granada' x 'Garden Party'), 1983

❧

This new introduction has a particularly lovely urn-shaped bud that spirals open into a symmetrical, recurved bloom. Each flower is a deep golden color, fringed with pink. Gold Medal looks much like a slightly smaller version of 'Peace,' with a darker yellow as its base. It isn't too surprising to find that 'Peace' is indeed in its lineage, as one parent of 'Garden Party.' The golden color deepens as the flowers age, while the pink edge finally disappears. Foliage is large and abundant, red to glossy green, and the plant is unusually hardy.

GRANADA

DONATELLA

HYBRID TEA
'Tiffany' x 'Cavalcade,' 1963

~

Granada is practically a tricolor rose, mixing sulphur-yellow, red and pink. The flower is only semi-double, but large and fragrant. It spirals open in classical hybrid tea fashion. Growth is very strong and healthy, and the big, bronze-green leaves are very resistant to diseases like black spot. It got a wopping 8.8 from the American National Rating.

GYPSY

HYBRID TEA

[('Happiness' x 'Chrysler Imperial') x 'El Capitan'] x
'Comanche,' 1973

❧

Another brilliant and luminous orange-red rose, like
'Mojave' and 'Granada,' Gypsy too has a name
meant to suggest the exotic. The flowers are not
large, but the bud is clean and ovate, appearing on
an almost smooth-barked cane with large, glossy
leaves. The contrast between bud and open flower is
particularly lovely in this rose, as its bud is colored a
dark red, nearly black.

HANDEL

LARGE-FLOWERED CLIMBER
'Columbine' x 'Heidelberg,' 1965

A very tall climber, Handel has for a pollen parent
one of the extra-hardy and vigorous roses known as
Kordesii climbers. Persisting in making crosses with
an almost sterile hybrid of *R. rugosa* and *R.
wichuriana,* the great German breeder Wilhelm
Kordes at last succeeded in producing a very fertile
and hardy plant, dubbed *R. kordesii.* This rose
became the parent of a whole race of hardy,
twice-flowering climbers. Handel puts forth copious,
middle-sized blooms with a marked fragrance. They
are creamy white, edged with pink and nested in
dark green foliage. The plant is so sturdy and
vigorous it received an 8.6 (excellent) from the
American National Rating.

HANSA

Rosa rugosa hybrid

Rugosa roses are much loved in their wild state.
They and their relatives have covered most of the
Northern Hemisphere for millenia, making them
welcome discoveries in waste places. Efforts to
incorporate their wonderful hardiness into hybrid
garden roses have met with mixed results. To some,
Hansa is an unfortunate failure; to others, it is a
wonderful success. Its groups of fragrant double
blooms repeat during a single season, and even
when these are gone, they are replaced by a mass of
lovely hips. The very prickly canes reach lengths of
almost 7 feet, lending the plant a pleasingly wild
effect. Those who despise the purple range in
roses—the mauves, the magnolias, the
magentas—detest Hansa, but they are just
being difficult.

HARISON'S YELLOW

Rosa spinosissima x *Rosa foetida,* 1830

Some say the cross noted above produced Harison's
Yellow; others claim it is just a sport, or mutant, of
R. spinosissima, the Scotch or Burnet rose.
Whatever the case, it was the first dependable yellow
rose to enter commerce. Within a few years of its
introduction—from the garden of G. F. Harison in
what is now mid-Manhattan, New York—the rose was
available from virtually all American and from many
European nurseries. Settlers spread the rose rapidly
through North America, so widely that today
historians can locate abandoned settlements just by
looking for surviving concentrations of the rose.
Harison's Yellow is probably the "Yellow Rose of
Texas" of the popular song. It bears masses of
intensely yellow, semi-double flowers on spiny canes
that grow gracefully to 6 feet or more. To this day, it
has few equals as a hedge or landscape rose.

IRISH GOLD
GRANDPA DICKSON

HYBRID TEA

('Kordes Perfecta' x 'Gobernador Braga de Cruz')
x 'Picadilly,' 1966

~

When you read enough rose names, you begin to
think that most modern roses are produced by a
coterie of septuagenarians who watch Lawrence
Welk and play the horses. Whoever they may be,
they are doing something right with Irish Gold, or if
you must, Grandpa Dickson. Its big, sweet-smelling
blooms are lemon yellow in color and are most
attractive in their oval bud stage. The bush's pale
green leaves make a delicate nest for this
tart, hot flower.

KING'S RANSOM

HYBRID TEA
'Golden Masterpiece' x 'Lydia,' 1961

~

Everything about King's Ransom is rich and large.
Its butter-yellow blooms, veined with darker yellow,
are as big as the bowl you may float them in: up to 6
inches across! The plant yields many of them, each
on its own strong, glossy-leafed stem. The fragrance
is powerful; the bush is more modest, however,
averaging 3 feet tall or under.

LILLI MARLENE

FLORIBUNDA

('Our Princess' x 'Rudolph Timm') x 'Ama,' 1959

~

Bright crimson, nearly scarlet, the blooms of Lilli
Marlene jostle each other in tight, vibrant clusters of
up to 30. Those who like full flowers will be
disappointed that these are only semi-double and
saucer-shaped, but their massed effect is as striking
as could be wished. The bush grows upright but
low—under 2 feet high—with red to green leaves,
lovely for the foreground of a rose bed.

Madame Hardy

Damask
1832

⌐

Damask roses are thought to have been made by joining musk *(R. moschata)* to Gallica *(R. gallica)* lines, but Madam Hardy probably has a touch of Centifolia—the once-famous Hundred Petals Rose—in it as well. In fact, it is sometimes classed, incorrectly, as *R. centifolia alba.* The large, ivory-white flowers are so dense with petals that they look more like camellias and so symmetrical they look as though they are the result of cutting some wonderful white ball in half. At certain stages, wisps of pink play around the petals' edges, and the fully open flower has a small green eye (really, its carpels) at the center. Madame Hardy always looks ruffled, but never mussed. She blooms only once, in summer, on a tall arching bush with gray-green leaves. If the canes bend too far under their load, it may be necessary to support them.

MARINA

FLORIBUNDA

'Colour Wonder' x seedling, 1974

~

From the Kordes nursery, one of the most prolific
hybridizers, comes Marina, a lovely, clean and
slightly strange floribunda. Its medium-sized orange
blooms, turning yellow at their bases, are fine
examples of their class, but they are borne singly or
in groups of only two or three, unusual for a
floribunda. The strong, upright bush nevertheless
puts forth numbers of long-lived flowers, each of
them very fragrant. The glossy, dark green foliage
sets the flowers off to perfection, making Marina a
lovely bedding rose. It is also a surprisingly good
cutting-garden subject.

MME. PIERRE OGER

BOURBON
'Reine Victoria' sport, 1878

The Bourbon roses originated with a chance cross, probably of *R. chinensis* and *R. gallica*, on the French island of Bourbon (now Reunion) in the Indian Ocean. From such sultry beginnings, one might expect a wilder flower. 'Reine Victoria' and Mme. Pierre Oger are fine names for these roses. Like Empire furniture or hooped skirts, they are full and rich, sensual in their own way, but they'll hardly recurve a petal to tell you so. Madame's flower is virtually globular, colored a creamy pink tinged here and there with lilac. Its China ancestor gives it the ability to bloom twice in a season, and the flowers stand out in clusters on a tall, rangy bush with shining green leaves. The only real drawback to this great Victorian rose is its susceptibility to black spot.

The Bourbon roses were losing out to their descendent, the hybrid perpetuals, even before Madame was introduced. She is among the few still available today. One other Bourbon still worth looking for is 'Souvenir de la Malmaison.'

MojavE

HYBRID TEA
'Charlotte Armstrong' x 'Signora,' 1954

In color, Mojave takes after 'Signora,' but it goes far beyond her. The name of the flower may be meant to suggest a desert sunrise...or a neon sign in the middle of nowhere. Colors like apricot, peach, carmine and salmon range across the petals as the flower matures. Each is borne singly on a long stem in a medium-high, glossy-leaved bush. Flowers are not double enough for some people's taste, but this means that the roses expose their eye-catching red stamens all the better. Mojave blooms make exquisite cut flowers.

MONTEZUMA

FLORIBUNDA/GRANDIFLORA
'Fandango' x 'Floradora,' 1955

～

Montezuma is a very vibrant salmon-red or carmine, its flowers perched in long-stemmed clusters at the end of tall, beautifully clothed canes. The blooms are up to 4 inches across, very large for a floribunda and arguing for the descriptive value of the alternative term, grandiflora, as a class. The flowers have hardly any scent, but what they may lack in fragrance they make up for in abundance. Each bloom in a cluster, except perhaps the center one, has a long enough stem to be cut for a vase.

New dawn

LARGE-FLOWERED CLIMBER
'Dr. W. van Fleet' sport, 1930

The average life of a modern rose variety is about five
years, the time it takes to reveal its deficiencies or
simply to be overwhelmed by improved novelties.
But New Dawn is still going strong after more than
five decades. It is a rarity in more ways than one.
'Dr. W. van Fleet' was an early success among the
first great contributions of the United States to rose
breeding—the result of crossing *R. wichuriana* with
tea roses. These crosses are very hardy,
strong-growing climbers that flower in attractive
clusters. A spontaneous sport, or mutation, produced
New Dawn, which has all the good qualities of its
parent, plus a quality then seldom found in climbers:
it blooms repeatedly. The full, 3-inch flowers are light
pink, springing out in clusters of up to ten. Grown
upright, it rises to heights of 9 feet or more, its long
canes weeping in graceful arches. It can also be
trained along a fence. One added advantage is
that the blooms appear on stems sufficiently
long for cutting.

OKLAHOMA

HYBRID TEA
'Chrysler Imperial' x 'Charles Mallerin,' 1964

⌁

From 'Charles Mallerin,' Oklahoma has inherited big, full flowers that are a dark, dark red. They are so deep in color that they can disappear into the green leaves surrounding them, but once you notice the blooms, they seem to draw you into their garnet depths. The cross has overcome the major fault of Oklahoma's pollen parent—its uneven growth. One fault remains: The flowers are so full, they will occasionally fail to open, their petals fusing across the tops and growing in tight, unsightly clusters until they drop.

OREGOLD
MISS HARP

HYBRID TEA
'Piccadilly' x 'Königin der Rosen,' 1970

❧

Oregold is an excellent yellow rose. The blooms are
large, solitary, golden, and supported on a vigorous
and leafy bush. A bloom will float like a rising sun
when placed alone in a shallow bowl. The plant is
not really hardy enough for climates where the
summers are muggy and the winters are cold.
Nevertheless, it was a 1975 AARS selection.

PASCALI

HYBRID TEA
'Queen Elizabeth' x 'White Butterfly,' 1963

~

Pascali is small, intense, perfect. Its formal, urn-shaped bud blossoms creamy white on a long cane, gradually spreading whorls of guard petals and opening into an elegant, pure white flower with just a hint of yellow at its base. The blooms are actually good-sized, packed with up to 30 petals, but they seem small because of the long, vigorous canes that bear them. Fragrant, prolific and set off by deep green foliage, Pascali is a wonderful cut flower, a striking standard, even a lovely choice for a patio container.

PEACE

GLORIA DEI

MME. A. MEILLAND

HYBRID TEA

('George Dickson' x 'Souvenir de Claudius Pernet') x [('Joanna Hill' x 'Charles P. Kilham') x 'Margaret McGredy'], 1945

~

Peace is the child of aged parents, but its beauty has bridged the century. 'Margaret McGredy,' the youngest of its progenitors, debuted in 1927, and the oldest of them, 'George Dickson'—a member of the now little-used class of hybrid perpetuals—appeared in 1912. Peace first bloomed in 1942 in the garden of French breeder Francis Meilland. It was smuggled to America in budwood form, and the rose received its most enduring name when it became the symbol of the 1945 United Nations conference in San Francisco. By any measure, it is still an extraordinary rose. The plant grows up to 4 feet high, thick with big glossy leaves. Flowers are cupped and enormous, borne singly on what are fortunately sturdy stems. Early on, the bloom is gold edged with pink. The pink reddens and the gold yellows as the flower ages, suggesting the dual pathos of flowers that deepen and flowers that fade. Peace is a bush or a bedding rose, and a fine supplier of cut flowers. It is hardy, but susceptible to black spot, and its fragrance is but slight. No matter. Well over 100 million plants have been sold.

PETER MALINS ROSARIAN

HYBRID TEA
'Crimson Glory' x 'Montezuma,' 1968

~

You will not find this rose in any catalogue or nursery. Peter Malins created it at the Brooklyn Botanic Garden over a period of eight years, and it can be seen there and nowhere else. A child of the deep velvet 'Crimson Glory' and the equally deep salmon 'Montezuma,' Peter Malins' rose reminds one that in every language that has a name for the rose, the name refers to the color—rose.

PIÑATA

LARGE-FLOWERED CLIMBER
seedling x seedling, 1974

~

This vigorous climber produces big double flowers that begin yellow with vermillion highlights, gradually turning all red as the blossom ages. Each bloom has fully 30 petals, and the bush throws out great clusters of them throughout the season. Leaves are dark with a matte gloss.

PINK PEACE

HYBRID TEA

('Peace' x 'Monique') x ('Peace' x 'Mrs. John Laing'), 1959

~

The great French breeders of the Meilland family
crossed 'Peace' twice into the lineage of this rose,
but it is 'Mrs. John Laing' that seems to have won
out. The flowers are not quite as mammoth as those
of 'Peace,' and their color is a smoky rose pink,
much like 'Mrs. John Laing.' Also like its paternal
grandfather, the bush has an old-rose fragrance that
is all but overwhelming. Like its progenitors, Pink
Peace is unusually vigorous. Some think that the
flowers are too loose and moppy; they are prejudiced.
The rose's studied nonchalance gives a lovely
pastoral effect, whether as a hedge rose or
as a specimen plant.

PROMINENT

GRANDIFLORA
'Colour Wonder' x 'Zorina,' 1970

～

Both of this rose's parents are rife with the pigment
pelargonidin, giving their flowers a bright,
translucent tone in the orange–salmon range.
Prominent outdoes them both in color, with buds
that are primary red on the petals' inner surfaces
and orange-scarlet on the outer. 'Zorina,' the pollen
parent, is a long-stemmed rose very popular in the
cut flower trade. Prominent inherits these stems, and
it, too, is a very handsome flower for a vase.
Fortunately, once cut it is also comparatively
long-lived. A cross between a hybrid tea and a
floribunda, Prominent has mainly hybrid tea habits,
but it is very floriferous and disease-resistant,
contributions of its floribunda parent.

PROUD LAND

HYBRID TEA
'Chrysler Imperial' x red seedling, 1969

~

Large, blood-red and prolific, Proud Land is a fitting
descendent for 'Chrysler Imperial.' The scented
flowers appear singly on long stems, colored a red
which is at once deep and relucent. The plant is an
unusually abundant producer of blooms, and its
growth is so vigorous that you had best cut the canes
far back when taking flowers for the house or
removing dead blooms.

QUEEN ELIZABETH

GRANDIFLORA/FLORIBUNDA

'Charlotte Armstrong' x 'Floradora,' 1954

❧

If you like ratings, you'll love Queen Elizabeth. She got a 9.0 in the American National Rating for garden value, which, modestly enough, means the rose is barely outstanding. There are few roses that win higher marks for color and form. The blooms grow in small clusters of up to five flowers—each a pure, soft pink—that start as high-centered buds and open into delicate cupped blooms. Late flowers look incurved, the broad outer petals cradling shorter petals inside, like an old Bourbon rose. The flowers last remarkably well when cut for the house. They must have plenty of space to grow. The vigorous bush easily reaches 5 feet, making it an excellent hedge rose. Its only real fault is that it has little fragrance.

ROSA MUNDI

Rosa gallica officinalis, sport

~

No, Rosa Mundi is not the famous York-and-Lancaster rose, supposedly the symbol of the end of the bitter Tudor feud, the War of the Roses. That one is *R. damascena versicolor,* a similar flower which is more fragrant but not so strikingly striped...and anyway, it probably only became the symbol apocryphally. Rosa Mundi is not described in botanical literature until 1581, but its origin is probably much more antique. It may have been brought from Syria by a returning Crusader during the twelfth century. Its common name is supposed to be derived from the name Rosamond (d. 1176), referring to Henry II's beloved mistress. In any case, Rosa Mundi remains a startling flower for the foreground of a bed. It grows low for an old rose—3 feet high at most—and it only blooms once each year, in late spring. But the medium-sized, 12-petalled flowers are bright and uniquely festive, with their white or light pink base boldly striped with red. The blooms open fully, revealing a nest of yellow stamens. Mildew may take the leaves later in the season, but it is worth the risk for those gay and courtly flowers.

ROSA RUGOSA ALBA

Rosa rugosa alba

Rugosa roses only bloom once each year, but they
will bloom almost anywhere. The plants have
survived winter temperatures as low as –50 degrees
Fahernheit! Originally from North Central Asia, the
species could be found in China and Japan as early
as the tenth century, and examples were catalogued
in the Empress Josephine's garden at Malmaison,
France, in 1814. Rugosas get around. And they can
grow into bushes taller than a man. Exuding an
intense fragrance, the lovely white, single flowers of
the *alba* variety are set among masses of small, dark
green and wrinkled (or "rugose") leaves. The
Japanese love the smell so much they mix rugosa
petals with camphor and musk to make perfume.

Stuffy ornamental gardeners think the dead
petals—which don't fall—are hideous, but they forget
the wonderful display of red rose hips that follows.

ROSA RUGOSA TYPICA

Rosa rugosa typica

This is the red form of *R. rugosa*. The term Typica is not botanically correct, but as the plant usually goes by that name, let's not fight. The clean, large single flowers with their contrasting buttons of stamens make this strong-growing shrub rose a good choice among those species roses newly popular in the landscape garden. Until recently, species roses had been comparatively neglected, since they tend to be messy and not good for cutting, and many only bloom once each season. (Perhaps these are faults only if you are addicted to hybrid teas.) The fact is that Typica will make a beautiful display of pentagonal blossoms all season long, even through a summer drought. After the flowers are gone come bright red hips and an autumn reddening of the foliage. The bush is advertized to reach 5 feet high, but it can top 8 feet, making it terrific for the background of a bed. If you are looking for still more shapely species-rose bushes, try the Caninas or the Spinosissimas.

ROSE GAUJARD

HYBRID TEA

'Peace' x 'Opera' seedling, 1957

'Opera' is a yellow-centered scarlet; 'Peace,' the queen of the hybrid teas, is golden with a pink tracery along its edges. The Rose Gaujard is carmine-pink on the inside of its petals and a sterling white on the outside. While this may not look like a textbook case for Mendelian genetics, it has nonetheless produced a striking rose. The very double, high-piled flowers are as much as a palm's breadth across and very fragrant. The plant is comparatively low-growing, but vigorous, remontant and disease-resistant. It also provides a good example of a breeder's own inbreeding: Jean Gaujard, its creator, is inheritor of the venerable Pernet-Ducher nursery. He was the breeder of 'Opera,' and the Pernet family is best known for the Pernetiana roses, the hybrids that brought true yellow into rose breeding. A 1926 Pernet-Ducher hybrid, 'Souvenir de Claudius Pernet,' is an important ancestor of 'Peace.' The Rose Gaujard's whole family tree is thus closely allied to its maker's professional family.

ROSERAIE DE L'HAY

Rosa rugosa rosea, sport
1902

~

It's purple. No question about it, though some catalogues pussyfoot around, calling it a dark velvety crimson...purple. No. It's bright purple. The blooms are large, loose and double, and they won't stop all summer long. Light green leaves set them off, on a healthy shrub that reaches about shoulder height. A striking and outstanding hedge rose, it takes its name from the famous French rose garden founded to recreate the Empress Josephine's even more famous one at Malmaison.

SPRING GOLD

FRÜHLINGSGOLD

Rosa spinosissima hispida x 'Joanna Hill,' 1937

Varieties of *R. spinosissima*—the Scotch or Burnet rose—have always been known as hardy climbers, excellent plants for the landscape. When the great breeder Wilhelm Kordes conceived the notion of hybridizing with Spinosissimas, he created a small group of hybrid Scotch roses whose excellence as tall bush or climbing roses is unsurpassed. Trained along a rail or with its canes arching in graceful forms, Frühlingsgold sends forth a mass of large, simple, well-shaped flowers, yellow to cream in color. They make a fine sight crawling all over the dense bush that may rise more than 12 feet high. The seed parent is a hybrid tea, and like that parent, Frühlingsgold will sometimes bloom twice in one season.

SWEET SURRENDER

HYBRID TEA
seedling x 'Tiffany,' 1983

～

The 1983 AARS trials winner for hybrid teas, Sweet
Surrender contains something old and something
new, all of it borrowed but none of it blue (or
magenta). The bushes have the vigor of the best
modern hybrid teas, sending up long stems
well-clothed with attractive foliage. It is very generous
with blossoms, bearing them usually one to a stem.
Both buds and blooms are high-centered and
shapely, colored a rose-pink that lightens towards
white. Though not too large, they are so packed with
petals that they may occasionally weigh down their
stems. The greatest delight, however, is Sweet
Surrender's musky, old-rose scent.

TIFFANY

HYBRID TEA
'Charlotte Armstrong' x 'Girona,' 1954

Tiffany is an archetypal hybrid tea. Like many of the finest of its class—including 'Chrysler Imperial'—it has 'Charlotte Armstrong' as one parent. Tiffany's buds are long and its slowly opening flowers quite large. The blooms are a salmon- to a deep rose-pink, nested in bases that tend towards golden. The flowers grow on tightly packed canes in a medium-high bush. Tiffany is so fine a hybrid tea that it received an 8.8 in the American National Rating, putting it at the top of the Excellent class. Its one atypical feature is a sweet one: its old-rose scent.

TROPICANA
SUPER STAR

HYBRID TEA

('Peace' x seedling) x ('Peace' x 'Alpine Glow'), 1960

To dispense with the qualifiers, Tropicana makes an
ungainly bush, and its foliage is comparatively
sparse. It is also prone to mildew and black spot.
This said, it remains a magnificent hybrid tea, a
close competitor with its double grandparent 'Peace'
for the honor of most sought-after rose. The color of
the flower is almost iridescent. An orange wash over
carmine pink, it sometimes tends to salmon,
sometimes to vermillion, according to light and angle
of view. The bloom, with its 35 petals, opens slowly,
holding its color and metamorphosing through
several enticing shapes. The flowers may appear
singly on a cane or in groups of two or three, each
having a pleasant fruity scent. Tropicana is perhaps
the finest rose yet created for the cutting garden. It is
Peter Malins' favorite. For all of its pedigree, however,
one of its key ancestors is well-known to residents of
the American South: *R. roxburghii,* the common
Chinquapin or Chestnut rose.

WHITE MASTERPIECE

HYBRID TEA
seedling x seedling, 1969

S. Eugene Boerner produced White Masterpiece at Oregon's Jackson & Perkins nurseries from two nameless seedlings. Simply put, it produces the shapeliest, largest and most elegant white rose known. Really a cream-white with greenish tints at the base, the flower blooms on a compact bush with lovely, dark green leaves. White Masterpiece does admirably in climates that approximate the temperate coastal areas of the American West, but it reacts poorly to hot, humid summers. Still, it is so beautiful one might even grow it in New Orleans, just for those first spring blooms.

ROSE GLOSSARY

AARS

The All-America Rose Selections (AARS) is a group created to test and evaluate the many new varieties of roses that are created each year. New roses are tested in 24 test gardens throughout the country during a period of 2 years, to evaluate their beauty, hardiness and disease-resistance. Less than 3 percent of the roses submitted receive the coveted AARS award.

BOURBON ROSE

A class of roses developed during the early and middle nineteenth century from what was probably a chance hybrid of *Rosa chinensis,* the remontant China rose, and *Rosa gallicax* or *Rosa damascena.* The flowers are semi-double to very double, often borne in clusters on compact bushes.

CALYX

A term referring to all the sepals of a flower as a group; the floral cup or receptacle.

DAMASK ROSE

One of the important ancestors of modern roses, *Rosa damascena* has origins that are lost in antiquity. It was already found in Egypt in Classical times, but was probably brought there from Asia. It was the first remontant rose known in Europe. The rose hybridizes easily and was used in the nineteenth century to produce the Damask Perpetual, or Portland, roses. In fact, they were seldom remontant—since the gene for repeat blooming is recessive and requires several generations to appear dependably—so they were soon replaced by more complex hybrids called hybrid perpetuals, which are themselves ancestors of modern hybrid teas.

DOUBLE

Said of a rose whose flowers average 20–40 petals each.

FLORIBUNDA

A class of modern roses first created by crossing polyantha roses with hybrid teas, producing a hardy, remontant bush rose with striking clusters of flowers. Used chiefly as bedding or hedge roses.

GRANDIFLORA

A name developed to describe the taller and more vigorous of floribundas. Both flowers and plants are usually larger than those of the floribundas, and the flowers may be shaped more like hybrid tea flowers.

HYBRID PERPETUAL

A class of roses, usually featuring very large double flowers, made by complex hybrids involving *Rosa chinensis* and many species of old shrub roses. Some of the varieties were remontant, and all had the now-prized old-rose scent. Developed chiefly in France during the latter half of the nineteenth century, they were eventually superseded in popularity by their descendants, the hybrid teas.

HYBRID TEA

The dominant class of modern roses, first bred in the early nineteenth century by crossing varieties of *Rosa chinensis* hybrids known as tea roses, with other hybrid roses of the time, particularly hybrid perpetuals. Hybridizing with varieties of *Rosa foetida* at the turn of the century produced the first modern yellow rose. Hybrid tea blooms tend to be large and shapely, usually borne singly on the long stems of a comparatively sparse bush. Their "tea" scent is usually much lighter than the musky scent of the old roses.

IMBRICATED
Overlapping, as though shingled.

OLD ROSE
Old roses are officially those which belong to a group existing before 1867 (a date that coincides with the introduction of the first popular hybrid tea, 'La France'). They include the moss, China, Noisette, Bourbon, Portland, tea, and Boursault roses, the *Rosa foetida* hybrids, hybrid perpetuals and early Spinosissima hybrids, plus the species roses.

POLYANTHA
Remontant roses first created in 1867 by crossing *Rosa chinensis* with a Japanese introduction, *Rosa multiflora*. They produced flowers in low-growing clusters and are important ancestors of the floribundas.

REMONTANT
Blooming more than once in a season.

SEMI-DOUBLE
Said of a rose whose flowers average 10–20 petals each.

SEPAL
Each of the parts of the calyx. Almost all roses
have five sepals.

SINGLE
Said of a rose whose flowers average 5–10 petals each.

STAMEN
The male organ of a flower, usually consisting of a stalk
called the filament, with a bulbous organ called the anther
at its top. In roses, their number varies from around 20 to
100 per flower, according to variety.

STANDARD
The tall rose that results when a bush rose is budded on a
tall understock; sometimes called "tree rose."

NOTES